SOLACE

SOLACE

Poems from the Northwoods

PATRICIA KILLELEA

Solace: Poems from the Northwoods copyright © 2025 by Patricia Killelea

Anspach Hall
Central Michigan University
Mount Pleasant, MI 48859
cmichpress.com
ISBN 979-8-9910646-2-0 (paperback)

Library of Congress Control Number: 2025936209

Interior design by Megan Monroe, with assistance from Bee Bielak and Janessa Shepard. Images by Lydia Geigle.

Grateful acknowledgment of editorial and production work done by the students of spring 2025 ENG 513.

Front cover design by Autry Clark. Front cover photo by Robert Hennesy. Back cover illustration by Khaneeros.

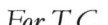

For T.C.

Table of Contents

SOLACE: *Poems from the Northwoods*

I. BOREAL JUNK MAIL

II. THE BALLAD OF LITTLE BONES

Table of Contents (cont.)

At some point in life
the world's beauty
becomes enough
—Toni Morrison

I.
BOREAL JUNK MAIL

DRIVING HOME ON U.S. 45 NORTH, YOU RETURN TO WHAT SHINES

This is for you who remembers the coniferous.
Who can take me to the places where trillium
dot the hillsides like ellipsis. Whose face rhymes
with plucking thimbleberry from the mountainside.

> Now this is for your heartbeat, its rhythm
> throbbing like sap inside a great tree.
> And this is for that sap you'll boil & bring
> to my lips so I can savor life's sweetness.

This is for you, because no one knows
how your voice glows like an ember,
feels like the sun on my face in the house
of winter when spring is still far off.

> This is for you, because you wash down
> each kiss with mouthfuls of Lake Superior
> even if it means spitting up shipwrecks
> for the rest of your days.

If we ever were separated,
you would find me by echolocation.
If I ever fell beneath the ice, you would call up
the muskies & they'd float me to the surface.

This is for you, because even the crows
stop to laugh at your dumb jokes,
leave feathers behind in the field
as gifts when no one's looking.

And now those crows in the sugarbush say
the secret to love is to keep what shines.
Tend to that good light. Leave the rest behind.
(Hasn't anyone ever told you all this before?)

This is for you because you shine.

POSTCARD: *GREETINGS FROM LAKE SUPERIOR*

They say this mouth of the river is hungriest
but nothing here is safe to eat. According
to the guidelines, according to the sheen.

They say, too, you can feel *convergence*
come sunset—how everything finds
its way into the lake, eventually.
You & I found our way here, didn't we?

> And maybe it's just the light, but from this shore
> the smelt look like they're shedding scales
> one by one. They scatter toxic trails leading
> back to us, but no one owns up to the shine.

> I know you believe in the goodness
> of this world, but me: I'm not so sure.
> That's why I'm reaching out.

You keep turning the postcard over in your hand
but you can't seem to find the right angle.
The one that shows you the way things really are.

Downstream, children splash in the stamp sands.
Cut toes on the slag. And upstream, forever
chemicals that never break down

are dividing the waters in two

      into   here is the darkness we can see
      &   here is the darkness we can't.

Still, I'm glad you came. I've been wanting
to show you this place for some time.

Families walking at dusk along the inland sea.
The first shooting stars with tails of glowing ore.
Waves we still love, the poison we can't stop calling home.

Someone tries to take a picture, but there's not enough light.
Someone says it's getting late, and it is.

      I'm sorry, but there's no hero in this story.
      No one arrives to save the day.

      There is no day to save,
      only the night,
      which saves itself.

PUT THIS DOWN & PLANT MILKWEED INSTEAD

There was a monarch in the radiator when they pulled up in the old GMC. Its spotty wings were flapping in the wind, so for a moment it looked like there was still a chance. But upon closer inspection, what it really looked like was a lie. That wasn't the first time. Earlier that day, a honeybee got sucked into the window, accidently stung the armrest. Now it's dying on the dashboard, all to the sound of the radio. Sometimes I arrive there too, asking questions. What if the song that's on right now is the last song you'll ever hear? Or this the last poem you ever read? At first, that puts pressure on things, but it doesn't need to be that way. Death could pull up at any moment, honk the horn, and that's it. You're walking out the door & you don't bother grabbing your keys or your phone or anything at all since you won't be coming back. Pockets lighter with all that not knowing.

> But you—you're not done yet. You're not
> stuck in a radiator, you're no set of broken
> wings. You could go outside & plant these seeds.
> You could even change the station. Or turn
> everything off & float around inside the silence.
>
> What you do with this information is up to you.

8

ON THE OCCASION OF YOUR HIBERNATION

One must have a mind of winter
—Wallace Stevens

I've been looking everywhere for you: I thought perhaps you'd
fallen beneath the ice but I couldn't find any cracks. So I kept
searching and came upon a nest filling (flake-by-flake) with snow.

> I was certain I'd finally found you there, below
> the rime. Instead, you were here the whole time:
> knee-deep in the drifts, trying to coax a word
> too shy to come out of hiding.

> Still—I understand your unrest.

The winters here can be so long. Like there's never enough
light to go around. But the glint on the pine says maybe there
is. Enough light. And once you hear the bones of your old life
snapping in the wind,

> there's nowhere to go but beneath the snows.
> Deep into the sleeping guts of quiet.

> So that's where I'll meet you.

We'll slow down our heartrates ((barely a beat/barely a chime)) and together ride out the cold.

                   But until then: like all the good animals
                   we'll practice our silence.

Yes, it is an art.
Only fear can teach you.

THE MIDDLE OF NOWHERE

I don't believe in the middle of nowhere—
every somewhere is a someplace to someone, every pine
a pine marten's favorite place for stashing kill,
every bright stand of goldenrod a gateway for deer
leaping between this world & the next.

When someone says we live in the middle
of nowhere, I want to remind them that this place
has many names: some dispossessed, some yet
to be spoken. But never was it not called a home—
which is the opposite of a nowhere, don't you think?

And when I hear voices repeating
the lie of nowhere,
I think of all the sandhill cranes
who return each spring to these same reeds
then take off before the frost weighs down the wing.
They don't believe in the middle of nowhere, either.

I guess all this middle of nowhere talk
is weighing on my mind because it's easier
to clearcut a place when you don't consider it a place,
so easy to carve out the belly of a mountain
until it's hollow
when you don't see it as a somewhere
                    with a heart or a center

But there is always a center, always.

So let's cease this middle of nowhere speak
and summon the center of somewhere speak.

As in   somewhere,   a wild strawberry
goes unpicked & bleeds   its sweetness
back into the earth,   a promise of summer
waiting for your tongue on the other side
of a hard winter.

As in   somewhere,   a moose
blends in with the road at dusk,
and from the corner of your eye
looks like the forest come alive
on four legs & you are never quite the same.

        And in the center
        of our deepest somewhere,

        Lake Superior swaps
        its sparkling calm
        for sudden rage,   pulls all in its path

                    down
                        down

into the coldest

below—

Now tell me again this is nowhere.

Tell me, so I can show you a place
so cold and deep, so dark & free
a place that already knows   your name
and is waiting.

MISSED CALL FROM THE MYCELIAL NETWORK

The bullet-holed STOP sign & the bumblebee
queens awaiting spring in leaf litter piles.
The ghost town at Robbin's Pond
& the smoothness of a blue-bead lily.
The wolf spider in her rusted beer can house.
A fire ant carrying the dead in its mandibles.
Fungal webs. Me & my failed rhubarb—

It's been a while.
Ages, even.

Hope we hear from you soon.

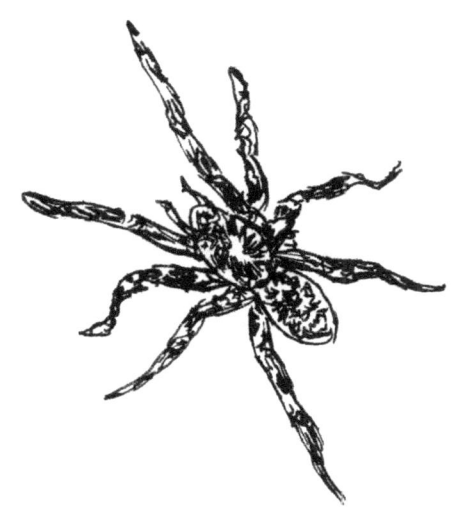

A FANTASTIC JOURNEY
IN THE NORTHWOODS

Once the ice melts, I will swim upriver
to the stamp sands and never turn back.

But I will wait for you to catch up to me,
wait there in the shallows laced with copper veins.

Maybe then we'll join the brook trout
& stroke the red stripes on each other's bellies.

Or we'll find other ways to breathe underwater
& we'll never have to call into work ever again.

One day if someone comes looking for us,
we'll hide in the shadows of basalt & shale.

Perhaps we'll outsmart an osprey, or trace
metals might leach into our organs

and we'll poison a mean old man
and laugh together secretly the way fish do.

Maybe the end of someone's hook will find us
but that won't be the end of our story—

What if your speckles are the last thing I see
as you leap out the fisherman's bucket.

      Or the last thing I'll hear is your falling
      with a slap back to the waves. Free.

In any case, don't stop swimming
until you've made it past Burned Dam.

      Swear then you'll burp a bubble up
      toward the world of air & sunlight.

In memory of my grin, its little sheen.

      You see, this life has been good enough for me.

CAPTAIN'S LOG 46°52'38.8"N 89°19'38.6"W

Restless night beneath the northern lights again.
Their activity seems to affect the whole system.

Even northern flying squirrels dream of rippling
skies somewhere high up in the tamaracks

And the coyotes slow their search
for smaller things in the crusted snow.

I feel like a small thing too & now the horizon
shifts directions to swallow me whole.

Who knows?—I might just let myself be taken.

Drift up to the green wisps
and pink ribbons diffusing above us.

The branches below would nod in agreement & all
the mottled snowshoe hares turn white instantly.

I suppose only a fool would speak of such things
which is why this will be my last entry.

BOREAL JUNK MAIL

Lately moths tend the porchlight like an all-night vigil.
Let's hope the cold snap doesn't freeze their powdery wings.

*

The crow walked up the porch steps and took
the dead starling from the welcome mat.

*

Would you like to hear a secret?
That's not powder on their wings but tiny scales.

*

Plant catnip if you want to keep the deer away.
Plant deer if you want to attract wolves.

*

Your attention, please! The first raspberry
of the season is not for human hands.

*

Forest roads lined with trillium. Forest roads lined with trillium.
Forest roads (marked for logging operations) lined with
(critically endangered) trillium.

*

The beak of a crow is a craw. So, in retrospect,
the craw was used to lift the dead from the welcome mat.

*

Those hardwoods on the logging road? Chopped down for paper.
It is the same paper you're holding now.

*

Long-horned bees are landing upon this word & the next.

19

They can see colors we can't; they detect ultraviolet poems.

*

(I regret to inform you that the cold snap
indeed froze all their powdery wings.)

*

Don't weed-whack raspberry canes when black bears are watching.
They won't forget what you took from everyone.

*

It's OK if you don't care about any of this.
There will always be more moths, more porchlights.

*

Just remember that next time you come around
asking the earth for anything.

DINNER DATE WITH A LAKE STURGEON

1. Something is moving beneath the ice. Something
a sturgeon once said.

2. Something like a song hummed once then forgotten,
or something striped like agate, twice as hard.

3. Something says the shoreline remembers mammoths
feasting the understory. Or something is fossilizing
even now, slipping between ages like tributaries.

4. Something to chew on. A sliver of history between
bony plates. Hardly any sturgeon remain in Sturgeon
River. As of this writing. As of this waterbody.

5. Something raises our beach glass. Here's to spawning
cleaner shoals. 150 million more years of returning
to the shallows.

6. Something stands in the way.

7. And beneath the ice again: traces
of the ancients stir. Shaking their barbels.
Eyes bulging black moons.

AN OFFERING TO SPRUCES

Now is the polar vortex and cold is king.
It wears a crown of icicles inside the flurry.

The light is unbearable, yet it must be borne
when winter holds a mirror up to memory.

This light remembers everything you've kept secret—
whispers piled up underground in burrows.

It is all the cries you've ever worn,
perfect flakes of snow melting in your dark hair.

The little droplets they leave behind
soak into the mind, which approaches stillness.

But still the persuasive cold settles around your tongue,
and the spruces, heavy with frost, lean down to listen.

II.
THE BALLAD OF LITTLE BONES

IN THE SUMMER OF 2020, WE PICKED BERRIES

When the cities began to burn, we picked berries.
It was either that or watch the sweetness spoil.
There's no stopping such things; I mean, the burning.
That summer, no one touched. We masked
loneliness with pixels but the traces never left.
Some families left family in sick-rooms & cried.
Others lied & some wrote poems because they still
believed in language. The rest counted bullets.

The only words that mattered were the headlines
& the names the names the names. Even here
in the woods, we could feel our country burning.
Got burned ourselves in ways we'll never say.

And maybe you didn't notice, but that summer
they came for the trees. Rows & rows marked
for felling. (Someone's always marked, you see).
Folks were running & afraid of running
out of toilet paper. Whole stands had to go because we all
had to go. The pines & firs. The maples & oaks.
Like so many things, it hurt to watch, so we stopped watching.
And then the forests themselves looked away.

We were still asking pines for forgiveness
when the flowers fell & it was time to gather.

On the news, the fear was getting louder, so we kept on
picking berries. Because the old folks would still need
their jam. But most of all, we needed something to keep us
from dreaming the war they all said was coming.
No matter how many jars we filled.

Alone as we were in the bush, I swear
you could feel the ripples coming—
sense a violence boiling across the backroads,
all the way to the berry patches. Deep in the roots.

Really, it had been here all along & everyone knew it.
Like the forests, we tried to look away.
But whenever we held up our hands, they were stained red
just the same.

ASTRAL PLANE Q&A

Q: *Global markets are increasingly unstable. What are your plans for when the U.S. dollar is no longer the reserve currency?*

A: I plan to unfurl
c a r e f u l l y

        like cedar buds
shy

        from the nibbling
of does.

Q: *How do you decide when a poem is finished?*

A: I write because it feels like someone close to me
is ~~dying~~ being born. I write because I think it's me.

Q: *Why should we hire you for this position?*

A: At the moment, I don't fit anywhere.
Even today I grew out of my house—
one hand on the latch, the other
smashed through the back window.
Cut my voice on the broken glass.

Q: *Are you aware that Nature Writing as a genre is problematic?*

A: There is one two-headed turtle for every 1,000 hatched.
      The heads fight, but usually one head is dominant.
      If one head dies so does the other.
      They share one heart, one circulatory system.

Q: *Where do you see yourself in five years?*

A: Even if the empire crumbles
      my tulips will do just fine.

WAIT & SEE

1.

Panfish don't have eyelids, so they can't close their eyes.
Meanwhile, bears have two: an upper & a lower.

The bears, the bluegill, the human:
All three of us see the cosmos in full color.
All of us are hungry for something
and biting down hard at the end of days.

2.

If you come across a ghost town
at the bottom of a pond,
you will be gifted with the language
of fins, the brightness of scales.

But you should always save the guts.
That's what makes the garden grow.

3.

Tomorrow we'll catch a few more.
Poems? No, bluegill—
even if both contain little bones.

Careful when you swallow them down.

4.
Dusk. Something compels me to look out the window.
There is an unusual darkness.
There between the fishing boat & the shed.

A new darkness is a useful mystery.

This one moves like shadow on shadow.
This one has four legs like my favorite memory.

5.
There's a bear in the yard, I say.
Where?   There. In the dark moving in the dark.
Drawn to the scales clinging to the bucket.

Whatever you leave outside isn't yours anymore,
if it ever really was.   It all goes back to the bush.

6.
Only a few smoked fish left in the freezer.
Still, if you come to my table, I will share what I have.

I can't help it—remembering what it's like
to go hungry. It changes you.

7.
I hereby apologize for having a dream
in which I came across wolves eating

your body & I joined them.

It was a very stressful time in my life.

8.

Early spring, so I'm digging up dandelion roots.
They grow best where I scattered the scales.
Roots for roasting & grinding for tea.
Good for the guts & gallbladder.
These days, people don't trust the roots of things.
A doctor's ideal, but what if they can't be reached?

I worry there might come such a day.

9.

That's what happens when you don't turn away.
You put a few more fish in the freezer.

Then your voice becomes the riverbed.

10.

Midsummer on Imp Lake: casting lines, looking for signs.
I'm energized by the sun and the hue of wild sumac.
If you stand near me long enough, I'll hand you a mason jar.
After a few sips, you'll taste like lemonade & tiny flowers.

11.
You could put these words in a jar (they'll never expire).
You could bury them under a column of basalt (volcanic).
You could call the bear & the bluegill, then wait (& see).

12.
Somebody is tearing up the roots again
with their claws, with their teeth.

13.
At dusk, back on the water, surfaces ripple
from hunger, which is a kind of disturbance.
And down by the edges, silt darkens
what once seemed so clear.

THE BALLAD OF LITTLE BONES

Last night I was walking the acid bog
& fell face-first into a pitcher plant.
They don't usually grow this large
but this one was ravenous, upright
& open-mouthed for centuries.
                    Wriggling

didn't do much—I was sticky
in body&mind, exhausted from years
of trying to say all the right things.
Cold-hardy, carnivorous, a northern
pitcher plant was something worth
surrendering to, I supposed.
Its waxy bloom. Its veined hollow
a portal to anywhere else but here.
                    So, like any ant

or fly, it took just 9 days to absorb me.
Such by the time you finish reading this,
my voice will be replaced with enzymes.
You'll be pleased to know it's really
not so bad here in the bog.
See, when it comes to beauty
I have always
                    been the prey.

BOBCAT EPIPHANY IN A TOTAL ECLIPSE

I stepped out of midday
into the belly of a bobcat.

Offered him a Black & Mild
because the tip is so sweet.

Everyone was looking, so the sun
took a smoke break behind the moon.

I felt so tired suddenly & napped
right there inside the bobcat.

Like any predator: my eyes are
forward-facing. Which means

I don't need special glasses to see.
How each of us casts our own dark

shadow across something or other.
At least once in a lifetime.

It all happens so quickly.

And with that, the bobcat yawned.
I crawled out of my old life

one ordinary revelation at a time,
put my smoke out on a stone.

I looked around once,
then walked into the firs

trailed by my little cloud.
Thankfully, I was never seen again.

NECTAR FROM THE SUN

Dawn. A sound of buzzing wings approaching from some-
where. Unseen. You stumble across a soggy mattress. Rusted
springs abandoned in the jack pines. Your favorite color: that
reddish-brown. Corrosion. Now, what are you going to do
with all these chemical reactions? Are you planning to oxi-
dize right here, in front of God & everybody? That's what
happens in the Iron Range. It can't be helped. Still—there are
meadow roses. Wild & vining in the metal scrap

which is one way to learn about history. Here's another.
Lesson 1. The world never stops repeating pointless cruelty.
There's no use in not fighting back. So dry your eyes. Plant
purple potatoes. Try to find your best lighting. Northern
Lights. Headlights. Red eyes of whippoorwill. Here the forest
floor is covered in red & green shotgun shells. Do you know
where you are? Lesson 2. Your phone wants

to autocorrect "crocus" with "crisis" & other warning signs
of spring. By now, you're so tired of being earthed & un-
earthed. Who else comes seeking refuge from memory? Like
tossing puzzle pieces into the fire. The way they melt and
peel. A message just for you. Recall licking envelopes for the
thrill of a papercut. Copper taste. See how talk of cutting
tongues conjures a wince? That's power. Spread the word.
Lesson 3. Thank you for your consideration, but there's no
refuge from memory. Just a junk pile

overcome with wild roses. Here's a late frost. Too bad for
tender shoots. But now you have a decision to make. Quick-
ly—while your voice is still in velvet. In this season of culling

self-doubt. For once in your life & for instance: that thought has antlers so it can be taken. This one has doe eyes so it can stay. Is this healing? Asking for a friend. Lesson 4. Put your ear to the sky. Listen. Mississippi Flyway

overhead. Scaup in migration speaking in tongues. A sense of lightness. Expansion. Your insides suddenly filled with white feathers. But that's never enough. You know what's coming. History with all its puzzle pieces. So instead? Swallow the afterbirth of these dark times. Chew up the pain. Turn it into more reasons to never surrender. Lesson 5. That's the spirit. But maybe the dark wants a little something

to remember you by. So you borrow entrails from a pine snake. Mix them with the streaking light of the Perseids. Add laugh tracks to your trauma. Hunker down for the oncoming storm. The ache of self-awareness. Thunder cracks & fallen tamaracks. The way lightning strikes strike fear in the heart of the overgrowth. Hence reduce paths to canopy. Control your burns. Learn how to regulate your nervous system. Last lesson. Life's a downpour but it's worth it. Sober. Pay attention by checking

your mailbox every day. Postcards from the future. From intuition. Bloody tongues & sky. Keep checking for new lessons. Even when you're nearly rusted. Or longing for numbness. You should lean in. Instead of away. A little sliver on the horizon. Just enough light. Just enough wild roses. And don't forget to look up every now and again. Otherwise, you'll miss it. Dawn. A hummingbird drawing nectar from the sun.

HUM

Sorry I didn't respond to your email.

Instead, I was somewhere in the cedars
arranging branches in my hair like antlers.

Please consider these tracks leading off
into the swamp my away message.

On second thought, it might be better
if you burned this book of poems,

left me in the liverwort where I belong.
I promise it's nothing personal.

Truth is, I love all beings better from afar:
wolves & stoats, humans & hawks.

One would gladly tear you to pieces
and the others would solemnly watch.

Why bother labeling which is which?

In the evenings, I sharpen
my teeth and hum a little song.

OUR HANDS HAVE BRIEFLY HELD
THE ANCIENTS

On the ATV trail, baby snappers wander all soft.
Newly hatched, it takes time for the hard shell to form.
Until then—there's not much that can be done.

Hence their coin-sized bodies scattered on the planks.
Good grub for the crows, who are always watching.
But a few still stir, so we come off our machines, lean low.

Life is filled with moments like these, glimpses into
a curious world we're a part of but can't stop fucking up.

Today it's scooping tiny snappers into our gloved hands.
Carrying them one by one from the bridge to the river.
Releasing each into the reeds & watching them swim on.

The further they move into the deep, the further
we drift into the quieter parts of ourselves.
Then we hop back on our quads, ride the dust back home.

I read somewhere that snapping turtles can live 100 years
or more. Which means, by now, the ones who survived
are tough-jawed & sharp-clawed, all battle-hardened.

But since then, I've only grown softer. Should I apologize

for that? Should we have left them there to die? Should we
un-fuck up the world when we get the chance or should we
look the other way? Should we get harder because life is hard
or should we open our hands—

When we say there's not much that can be done,
do you really believe that?

RARE EARTH

These elements are not especially rare, but they tend to occur together in nature and are difficult to separate from one another
        —Oxford Languages

1.
Before I said it aloud, I hid
my feelings for you beneath a bed
of frozen sphagnum moss.

But now I'm ready to kiss you
with lips as red as the dogwood
in winter.

My love stands out bright against the snow.

2.
Now the light returns a little more each day.
Soon, we're kneeling together in damp shade
trading a promise between wild leeks.

There's something ephemeral about us
that must be harvested carefully.

3.
Come ceremony, the ash burl
stood watch, the lady ferns, too.

Who needs rings when the green
is this green, when nearby the walleye
leap up & slap their tails, sealing the vow?

4.

We sleep surrounded by swamp tea.
And we wake to cranes bugling
to one another at the river's nesting edge.

When I think of them wrapping their long gray
necks around each other, I am quiet again at the root.

5.

The cranes & the swamp & two lovers standing very still:
something to do on earth a little while, anyways.

6.

Season after season—have you heard
the humming sound that fills the air
all around us? Between the trout lilies.

Floating forever inside that sound:
that's my idea of heaven, if you care to hear about it.

7.

No, that doesn't feel like the right word.
Instead, let me show you my favorite blueberry patch.

8.
When you detect the wings of luna moths
brushing your cheek like tiny tongues, just know

I want to be the wings I want to be the tongues
I want you to hold me like the cranes like the wild
leeks & the nesting edge.

9.
I want to find out if this strange
life was worth all the trouble
because I'm beginning to suspect it was.

GREAT LAKES SENTIMENTAL

When the rain washes you clean, you'll know
—Stevie Nicks

For years, I was the hard tooth

of the sea lamprey
but now I'd go to war
for my tenderness.

That's why I come bearing gifts:

>   Asters bursting
>   from my lips.

>   An armful of deer
>   apples for your pile.

>   Desire as wide as
>   the Sturgeon River Gorge.

Now my love & I are found

growing everywhere together
like wild blueberry
& sweet fern.

Sweet sweet without shame.

(If your heart's been dried
& split & stacked, you're free
to turn away—

> But as for us
> we were born to mourn
>
> & we're shining
> anyways.)

48

III.
NEXT LIFE

NOTE FROM YOUR SECRET ADMIRER
(THE POLAR VORTEX)

Look: I'm not looking
to give up all the secrets
of the woods.

> Truth is, they are not
> mine to give.

All I'm asking is for you
to take my hand

& keep on taking it

as we make our way deeper
into this January night.

> I promise the dark
> is just getting started.

WINTERKILL

Someone at the corner store spoke on the fish
bellied-up in the 100's—how they line the shores

       of inland lakes once the thaw takes over.
       Blame it on the ice.   If it's too thick:

oxygen dwindles & the suffocation begins.
But you never know until spring.

       Come ice-out, they float up to the shining

surface one last time. Relic to a season trapped
beneath the freeze.

       They call it winterkill.

I said that must be a sight to behold, & the fisherman
looked me in the eye   said no,   it's not.

THEY'RE CALLING HUNGER *FOOD INSECURITY* NOW

Hunger has four legs and putrid fur—
I know it because I've run my hands
across the ragged length of it,

felt its sharp bones jutting into
my voice   Always hunger comes
pacing a few thoughts behind my own,
leaving imprints in the snow

Then picks up its step & bristles
in those last days before the end
of the world or the first of the month

      Hunger has a name I keep trying
      to forget, has a collar with a tag
      I keep trying to lose, but always
      its memory nuzzles against my own

      For hunger knows
      that even when cash flows, there's no
      filling up old starvations: armies
      of bellies that come howling down

      howling   Even when there's food

on our table forever now   All these years
with instead of *without*

Even when new children
are learning hunger as I write these words

Even as I begin filling my own bowl twice.

THINGS WERE GOING GOOD

So I decided to make a mistake. I shot up into the air like a
ghost from sleep. Brushed the car crashes from my eyes. I
had everything to lose & this pleased me. Naturally, I braced
for impact. Raised all my hackles. That night, my mother went
through the trouble of raising herself from the dead just to
tell me *You better watch your mouth*. So I've been up all night,
watching. Stirring the pot. Trying to fatten a whole alphabet.

There are over 17,000 vehicular accidents a
day. What if language is the vehicle on nights
like these, what if there's more than one way
to bleed out on the asphalt. Or maybe some-
one should jot this down to keep track of all
the spilling. Remember. They run in packs
foaming

at the mouth, so you're bound to hit one—a memory. Brace
for impact. Aren't you beginning to realize this was no mis-
take. We were meant to cross paths at just the right time.
When time stands still. Like a good dog: stay. Stay with me
until morning. We'll take turns stirring the pot. Haters barking
in the distance. They're uninvited to the fish fry.

Studies show that people asleep have higher
rates of survival in a crash. Should I both-
er waking you? Or would you like to go on

dreaming? Most of all: in an accident, things
really s l o w down. Tonight it feels like it's still
happening. Like we never stopped crashing.
Like we're still flying through history, locking
eyes before we crumple.

And now the dogs arrive, circling our final
breaths. Isn't this always the best part? The
arriving. Now it's probably time to set
the record straight. Start paying attention
to all these patterns.

Some thoughts come sniffing back around whether you want
them to or not. Since last we spoke, I'm pleased to report that
I've lost everything. Yes, it's all going according to plan. But
this alphabet's still hungry. I don't know how much more I
can take. Take a car crash, take a ghost story based on events
from your life. You play the ghost.

Which brings us to why we've gathered here.
The people want to know. What do we do
with all the stories we make up about the
people we love? Do we send them back to the
place they came from, gnawed to the bone?
It's hard to tell which part is the mistake.
The love or the gnawing. Harder still to tell
the difference between story and bone.

I think I've made myself quite clear. Words swirling in the
bone broth. Patches of memory like black ice. Dogs relaps-
ing to wolves once more. We should really be more careful.
Everything's an invocation, everything's a mirror.

Like my mother always said:
You better watch your mouth.

THIS SENTENCE IS GLUED TOGETHER BY PINE PITCH

First light: pileated woodpeckers eye me with suspicion.
It's spring & they keep a nestling nearby.

This season brings out the worst in us
despite all the awakenings.

They shriek at smoke from the fire in our yard.
I'm sorry, I say, but there's work to do, things to burn.

> I don't recommend setting such
> sorry excuses too close to the burn pile.

> Every time I do that, the whole sound
> of my life melts away, nestlings & all.

Can it be helped? Knowing how every fire
I light takes oxygen from something else.

Now I eye even myself with suspicion.

> Even if it's spring.
> Even if the spark of life's returning.

> Something must be fed to the fire.
> Might as well be me.

A RUSTED BIRDCAGE IN AN OTHERWISE EMPTY FIELD

When I first came across the field,
I was searching for you—
or was I searching for myself?
Back then, it was hard to tell.

I found a note near the cage
in my own handwriting.
There on the page:
a single word.

Suppose I can't get the taste
of that word out of my mouth.
Suppose I wake each morning,
unfold the paper again&again

trying to remember the reasons
why I kept on trusting you.
Despite the rust.
Despite the warnings.

Maybe it was because
I hated myself, as simple
as that sounds.
It took so many years to see.

What was I really doing
the whole time
I thought I was living?

Every time I ask that question,
I hear a ringing in my ears
        like I'm just about
        to wake up.

Until then, this is how
every poem of mine begins:

Wherever I go, I am the stranger.

THE RIVER KNOWS

Please believe me. The river told me
very softly: want you to hold me, ooh ooh ooh
                    —The Doors

If you must speak to me of rivers, you can't leave out
the drowning. That's the burden of remembering. How
in the evening, aluminum boats line the reedy shore,
churning the names of the lost in trolling wakes.

Later tonight, I'll drop a meadow rose into these murky
waters. Wouldn't you want the same done for you, too?
Should the river ever claim you? —A rose, at least, a word?

Now see how that word floats to the farthest bend, then
disappears from our choppy view. It happens so soon, doesn't
it? The disappearing. By the time you look up, the stars
& satellites are already out, flickering greetings or farewells.

Below, the muskies open their mouths like trap doors.

A FIELD GUIDE TO THE REAL WORLD

Every year a little
warmer, a little less
snow.

                  Mosquitoes
                  in January.

.

                  Maple sap
                  unsure
                  when to run.

If this goes on
no walleye spawn
when the ice breaks.

                  There won't be ice
                  to break.

                              (Something else
                              is breaking.)

Maybe fire & ash
borers take the last
of the grove.

Maybe the storm.
The toxic algae
bloom or flash flood.

The sea level replies
(There is no guide)

Every year a little
warmer, a little less
snow.

DISPATCH FROM *THE PAULDING LIGHT MYSTERY*

While we are sleeping, they gather at the top of the hill, dusty
from lack of rain, gather just the same to see some flicker
of green or red—white on a clearer night.

> Clearly the fuss is in the flickering, all eyes
> glued to the sky; but for us, who live beside
> *The Paulding Light,* it's more than a tourist
> attraction.

Sure, it's good for a few bucks a t-shirt keychain
magnet doohickey. They'll fill their gas at our station,
fill their phones with blurry pics. But best of all,

> Tourists bring fresh eyes. And such a strange
> light longs to be seen, doesn't it—otherwise,
> why glow? Five minutes away, you'd think we
> who call this place

Home would tire of the Light—would shake our heads,
dismissive of the glimmer and its campy lore.
But that's simply not true. Locals bear a healthy

> Respect for the shine, have their own takes on
> its origin. I know people who swear they've been
> chased by the orbs, who've crested the hill in
> the midnight hour to smoke a few

Blunts or knock a few back, just to drive back to town
earlier than expected, shaken. Shaken by the Light.
And the story goes like this: a railroad brakeman

> (Long ago when the valley was covered in
> tracks) held up his lantern each night to signal
> the trains. But two cars were stopped on the
> line & the man

Was struck stone dead trying to stop
the collision. Now he haunts the stretch
between that hill & Paulding proper,

> & it's his swinging lantern you see in the
> distance. Others say it's spirits, say swamp gas
> or the dance of some lonely ghost. Then, in
> 2010, investigators

Gathered at the top of the hill, dusty
from lack of rain, gathered just the same
to test out that story with instruments.

> They measured the distance, they measured
> time, even found a way to measure radiance.
> Their conclusion? Just headlights traveling
> on U.S. 45.

So they came & they left, wrung out
the phantom from the story, moved
onto the next. But faith's a far-flung

thing. Besides: some say the apparition still
appears on nights with no traffic, the hair on the
arm still stands straight up when the eerie glow
comes floating down fast.

And that red light? That red light moves
closer, until it hovers right on top of you—
tastes like fear or dust in the mouth.

Tastes like maybe you don't know everything
& maybe that's not so bad. Fog circling your
head as you hop in the truck to head back
home.

As for myself, I've seen what I've seen.

What I can say is this: when it comes to *The
Paulding Light*, the mystery isn't the illumination
itself, but in the holding. We all want to believe
that someone will hold a light for us

Out there in the darkness.
We want to believe in some shine
that can't be measured.

And while we are sleeping, they gather
just the same.

WHAT COMES NEXT

There is a café in the clearing.
Instead of cups and plates:
little bones and bits of fur
scattered all around.
These are the crumbs of life
and death: the true menu.

Over and again, the claws
and teeth come together
in prayer, repeating hunger.
Filling the ancient belly
with a Special of the Day,
something or someone.

A sign pinned to the jack pine
reads: *All the atoms you see before you
were made inside of dying stars.*

Now take a seat here in the loam
and let us make a toast.
For you too were born to grind
all this stardust down with molars.

You swallow & sniff around for more.
Then you step out into the clearing
and wait for what comes next.

POEM TO BE READ SHORTLY BEFORE MY REINCARNATION

Next life, I want to be the animal who comes
across her reflection in the waters & doesn't stop
to wonder whether or not it is beautiful

> Or next life I'll perch in the ash, try on black
> feathers & catch the falling leaves so I can glue
> them back to the branches

Maybe next life I'll become the albino deer
crossing ice sheets all winter to reach the promise
of spring on the other side

> Or next life, I'll find a way to use my whole body
> to speak in vibrations, like a spider or a cicada
> & I'll make candlelights flicker just to let you know
> i'm still around

Next life, I'll definitely have hooves made of agate
& I'll train my eyes to travel by birchlight, or I'll swim
from the stars all the way back to the river where I was born

It shouldn't be too hard to find me again

> Because in the next life, I'll become the first moth
> to finally reach the moon, the first flake of snow

to melt on your tongue

Will you meet me there too
Will you glow there beside me
Will you become the waters
I gaze into, or the ash

Will I find you again in the falling leaves,
or in the flicker, next life.

Notes

BOREAL JUNK MAIL–The line, "It is the same paper you are holding now," is a slightly modified line borrowed from Peter Richards' *Oubliette* (2001).

THE RIVER KNOWS–Title comes from the song, "Yes, The River Knows," by The Doors (1968).

THEY'RE CALLING HUNGER *FOOD INSECURITY* NOW–According to "Feeding America West Michigan," one in seven children in the Upper Peninsula of Michigan are food insecure.

Acknowledgments

All of these poems were written in Getegitigaaning in Anishinaabe-Aki. Support tribal sovereignty if you really love this land.

Thank you to the editors of the following journals where some of these poems originally appeared:

"Postcard: *Greetings from Lake Superior*"–Originally published in *Sky Island Journal*.

"An Offering to Spruces" and "What Comes Next"– Originally published in *Suisun Valley Review: 40th Anniversary Edition*.

"Poem to Be Read Shortly Before My Reincarnation"– Appeared as an audio feature on *The CryptoNaturalist* Podcast.

"They're Calling Hunger *Food Insecurity* Now"–Originally published in Saginaw Valley State University's Writing Program newsletter *Writing@SVSU*.

Some of these poems originally appeared as poetryfilms:

"In the Summer of 2020, We Picked Berries"–Official Selection for the *REELpoetry/HoustonTX: International Poetry Film & Video Festival*.

"A Rusted Birdcage in an Otherwise Empty Field"– Originally appeared as an online feature streaming at *FENCE*.

"The Middle of Nowhere"–Received Honorable Mention at *The Midwest Poetry Film Festival*.

Deepest gratitude to my beloved family, especially T.C. (who shines), Margarite Alves, Lisa McGeshick, all the cats. I couldn't do it without you. Always grateful to my mother, Shirley Osejo, gone all these years but never forgotten.

Thank you to Monica McFawn for helping me weather the storms. Shout-out to Adam Alves + Echo, Nova, and Mar–you are the future. Love always to Jaspal Kaur Singh, Christine Ami, Laurel Sexton, Emily Wallace Hughes, Aubrey Hess–true friends. Love to all the badass kids at LVD Boys & Girls Club. Big hugs to the coolest girls I know: Aly Klingman, Blessing Shively, Baby Char.

Thank you to Sarah Tremlett, Dave Bonta and all the video poetry artists worldwide who keep things weird & wonderful.

Thank you to Austin Hummell for reading the earliest version of this manuscript. Thank you to Diane Seuss for selecting this title for the Summit Series Prize, to Matthew Roberson & his students and Megan Monroe for their work at Central Michigan University Press. Heart to *Passages North* and *FENCE*, always.

My appreciation to the Department of English at Northern Michigan University, especially my colleagues in the M.F.A. program. Special thanks to my students who make it all worthwhile, especially Dez Brown, Lisandra Perez, Alex Watanen, Sara Daniels and Olivia Kingery. Thank you to my teachers throughout the years, especially Joe Wenderoth.

For this place. And for love, despite the odds.